Georgia TO GEORGIA

★ MAKING FRIENDS IN THE U.S.S.R. ★

Georgia TO GEORGIA

MAKING FRIENDS IN THE U.S.S.R.

by Laurie Dolphin

photographs by E. Alan McGee

TAMBOURINE BOOKS ★ NEW YORK

To my American family—Ben, Miles, and Brian—
and my Georgian friends

L.D.

To my son, Matthew—world peace is possible through friendships
that are created with the children of every nation.

E.A.M.

Text copyright © 1991 by Laurie Dolphin
Foreword copyright © 1991 by Paata Shevardnadze
Photographs copyright © 1991 by E. Alan McGee

Library of Congress Cataloging in Publication Data
Dolphin, Laurie. Georgia to Georgia: making friends in the
U.S.S.R. / by Laurie Dolphin; photographs by E. Alan McGee. p. cm.
Summary: On a visit to promote friendship and understanding
between Soviets and Americans, a young boy from Atlanta, Georgia,
observes life in the Soviet Republic of Georgia.
1. Georgia—Relations—Georgian S.S.R.—Juvenile literature.
2. Georgian S.S.R.—Relations—Georgia—Juvenile literature.
3. Georgian S.S.R.—Description and travel—Juvenile literature.
[1. Georgian S.S.R.—Social life and customs.   2. Soviet Union—
Social life and customs.]   I. McGee, E. Alan, ill. II. Title.
E183.8.S65D65   1991   303.48'273047—dc20 90-47494 CIP AC
ISBN 0-688-09896-7—ISBN 0-688-09897-5 (lib. bdg.)

Printed in the United States of America
Book design by Golda Laurens
First edition
1 3 5 7 9 10 8 6 4 2

Acknowledgments

The author would like to pay tribute to those who helped with the telling of this story:

The Schulten family, without whom there would be no story.

Lamara Margvelashvili and the children of School No. 53 who welcomed us so warmly.

The Georgians in the U.S.S.R. who generously took us into their homes and hearts—Iamze Machavariani, the Machavariani family, Lamara Esvanjia, the Tskitishvili family, the Bagrationi family, and the Shevardnadze family.

Tea Tskitishvili and Vakhtang (Buka) Esvanjia, Jr., who were our interpreters and guides during our visit and to whom I give special thanks.

Vakhtang Esvanjia, Sr., who understands that friendship is not limited by distance, age, or time.

Nugzar Ruhadze, Soviet-Georgian feature reporter for television station WXIA in Atlanta, who was an invaluable resource.

Finally I wish to thank Paulette Kaufmann, Golda Laurens, Willa Shalit, Mary Ann Shaening, Ron Pokrasso, Ben Dolphin, Fidea Bergen, Candy Jernigan, and Murray and Rita Stichman for their friendship and support throughout this whole project.

Foreword

People throughout the world search for peace and friendship. No matter what language they speak, their dreams, thoughts, and aspirations are almost the same. Sometimes it is only geographical distance that makes us seem different.

The book *Georgia to Georgia: Making Friends in the U.S.S.R.* shows how satisfying understanding between people can be, particularly when this feeling is carried by children. Boys from two very distant Georgias, American and Soviet, became friends and opened up a totally new world. Seeds planted in Soviet Georgian soil in tribute to American Indian custom have sprouted just like friendship between young men from the two countries.

Americans know very little about Soviet Georgia. This book, which is dedicated to children, is a successful attempt to introduce Americans to what Georgia looks like and how Georgians live. As a representative of my people, I should say that all the episodes and pictures in this little story are very typical of Georgia and reflect Georgians as one of the most unique and ancient peoples of the world.

PAATA SHEVARDNADZE

My name is Joe. I live with my family in a small town right outside of Atlanta, Georgia.

A couple of years ago my mother started a letter-writing campaign. She went to schools all over Atlanta asking students to write letters to children in the U.S.S.R. She hoped American and Soviet children could become friends, because when they were grown up they would be responsible for making and keeping peace in the world.

When Mom asked me and my sisters to be the first to write letters, we didn't think it was a good idea. "How can we trust them?" said my older sister Tiffany. "They have a huge army and bombs!" My younger sister and I admitted that we were also afraid of the Soviet Union.

My mother said we shouldn't be afraid of people we didn't know. "Your letters can make these strangers into friends!" she told us. And so Tiffany, Jenny, and I wrote our first letters.

For several months my mother collected letters and brought them home. She would read many of them to us.

Her favorite letter was the one from a girl in Atlanta who wrote about an ancient American Indian ritual. She explained that different tribes joined together to plant seeds with a feather to renew the friendship between their tribes. She enclosed a package of seeds to be planted on Soviet soil with the wish that as the seeds grew, friendship and understanding between the U.S.A. and the U.S.S.R. would grow too. My heritage is part Native American, so naturally I liked this letter.

One day my mom came home with great news. Our whole family had been invited to go to the Soviet Union as part of a delegation. We were headed for Tbilisi, the capital of the Republic of Georgia. It was a dream come true for my mother. Now she could take all the letters herself. I was going to carry the seeds.

My sisters and I didn't know where Tbilisi, Georgia, was so I found our atlas and looked it up on a map.

I could see that the Soviet Union is divided into fifteen republics the way the United States is divided into fifty states. Georgia, U.S.S.R., is a southern republic just like Georgia, U.S.A., is a southern state. But the U.S.S.R. is so much bigger, almost three times as big as the U.S.A. In fact it is the largest country in the world.

ВИЗА

К-II № 703632

ОБЫКНОВЕННАЯ

ВЬЕЗДНАЯ–ВЫЕЗДНАЯ –

Гр. США

Фамилия ШУЛТЕН

Имя, отчество АЛЛЕН
(имена)

Дата рождения 181178   Пол МУЖ

С детьми ОДИН
до 16 лет

Цель поездки КУЛЬТУРНЫЙ ОБМЕН

В учреждение ДЕТСКИЙ ФОНД ГРУЗ. ССР

В пункты ВАШИНГТОН, МОСКВА, ТБИЛИСИ

Действительна для въезда в СССР с 190490 19 г.,

пребывания и выезда из СССР до 270490 19 г.
через пограничные пункты СССР,
открытые для пассажирского движения

090490
Выдана 19 г.
042424351
К паспорту №

ВЫЕЗД

When anyone wants to travel to the Soviet Union they must apply for a permit to enter the country. This is called a visa. Our family had to wait for many months before our visas were approved by the Soviet government. When they finally came it was just one week before we were planning to leave. We were so relieved.

This trip was going to be my first one on an airplane and the longest one I had ever taken so I was a little scared. The farthest I had traveled before was from Atlanta to Colorado and that was by car.

On the plane I sat with Mom and Dad. I had the friendship seeds in my pocket. First we flew to New York. Then we flew for 9 hours and 4,569 miles to get from New York to Moscow. When we landed in Moscow we were now a quarter of the way around the world.

It was 5:00 P.M. in Moscow when we arrived but it was only 9:00 A.M. in Atlanta. There is an 8-hour time difference between Atlanta and Moscow. So my friends at home were just starting their school day while it was almost dinnertime for me.

At the passport control desk a soldier checked my visa. He carefully looked at me and then my picture several times. It seemed to take forever. Then he finally stamped my visa and we were free to go. We were officially in the Soviet Union.

But we still had more traveling to do. We drove to a smaller airport and took one more plane three hours south to Tbilisi.

By the time we arrived we were very tired and very hungry, but there were lots of people waiting to meet us. A young man handed me flowers and said in English "Hi, I'm Buka. Welcome!" I was surprised to hear him speak English. I expected to hear only Russian. Buka told me that he spoke three languages—Russian, English, and Georgian. "Georgia has its own language and its own unique culture. You will see. I will be your guide and show you everything."

I stayed with Misha Matiashveli while I was in Tbilisi. He lives with his parents and one brother in an apartment. Their apartment has a living room, a kitchen, two bedrooms, one bathroom, and a terrace.

Misha's mother made a huge dinner to welcome me. We ate *chikhirtma* (chicken broth and egg), *satsivi* (turkey in walnut sauce), and *pkhali* (vegetables and walnuts) and drank Tbilisi lemonade and Pepsi. While Misha's mother was serving dinner she repeated an old Georgian saying: "When a guest comes to the home it is like sunrise. When he leaves it is sunset for his host." It sounded like what we call Southern hospitality back home, only more so.

Misha shares his bedroom with his 21-year-old brother Merab who is attending medical school. Misha loves music. He has tapes of Michael Jackson, Sting, and Stevie Wonder. He even has a picture of Brooke Shields on the wall! I felt right at home.

On Monday Buka drove Misha's mother to the farmers' market to buy food for dinner. He brought along another boy for me to meet. His name is Shota and he is just my age.

The food in the market definitely looked different. The meat was not wrapped in packages and the spices filled huge bags. I saw suckling pigs arranged in rows and entire cows hanging from racks.

Buka told me that all the food in this market came from farms outside of Tbilisi. There is a lot of fertile farm land which produces citrus fruit, grapes, apples, and pears in Georgia. The Georgians produce almost all the citrus fruit and tea that the Soviet Union consumes and they are well known all over the Soviet Union for the wine that comes from their vineyards. Their southern climate is especially good for growing delicious peaches, just like in Georgia, U.S.A.

Misha's mother bought suckling pig to roast, beets, and salad greens. She paid with paper money and coins called rubles and kopecks. There are one hundred kopecks in a ruble. When we bought meat the man used an abacus to add up the price.

We needed bread for dinner too. So Misha's mother took us to a bakery where they make Georgian bread every day.

When we arrived at the bakery I noticed the sign. It said House of Bread in two languages, Georgian and Russian. Georgia not only has its own language, but it has its own alphabet too. This ancient alphabet, which has thirty-three letters, is one of the fifty living alphabets in the world. The Georgian language is as different from Russian as English is from Japanese.

Inside the bakery they make *shoti pori*. It was amazing to watch the bread being made. The clay ovens were so large you could stand up in them. When the fire at the bottom heats up the oven the baker throws the dough against the side to bake. When the bread is done the baker flips off the loaf and sets it aside to cool. Georgian bread smells and tastes delicious!

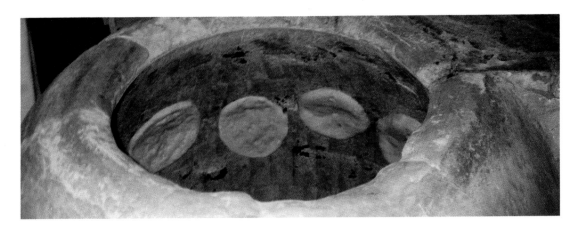

Buka drove us everywhere by car. I was surprised to see so many cars. There were even traffic jams. The cars are small and all look the same. There are only a few kinds of cars that you can buy in the U.S.S.R. Buka told me that people have to wait in long lines to get gas for their cars. Sometimes the wait takes over twelve hours.

Wherever we drove in Tbilisi we could always see hills and mountains. On one hill there is a very large statue called the Mother of Georgia. Buka explained that she carries a sword in one hand to fight off their enemies, and a bowl of wine in the other hand that welcomes their friends.

In ancient times Georgia was a separate country. But it was invaded all the time. The Persians, Romans, Arabs, Turks, and Mongols all were their enemies at one time or another. They wanted to rule over Georgia's fertile and wealthy lands. Tired of all the fighting, in 1783 they asked the Russian czars for protection. A few years later Georgia was annexed by the Russian empire. After the Russian Revolution of 1917, Georgia briefly regained its independence. Then in 1921 it rejoined what was now the U.S.S.R. and became a republic in 1936.

On Sunday Misha's family went to church. "Before Gorbachev we weren't allowed to go to church because the government prevented religious worship," Misha's father told me. "Now there is no restriction and we are happy."

Here the most common religion is Georgian Orthodox Christianity. The Georgians adopted Christianity in the fourth century, six hundred years earlier than the Russians. The Georgian Orthodox cross is covered with grapevines, which are a symbol of generosity.

Misha's mother showed me a synagogue, a mosque, and several Georgian, Armenian, and Russian Orthodox churches. She told me that Christians, Moslems, and Jews have all lived in harmony in Tbilisi for many years.

During the week I went to school with Misha every day. His school day starts at 9:00 A.M. and ends at 2:30 P.M. He attends the first shift. His best friend starts school at 3:00 for the second shift. Misha has been going to the same school, called a high school, since he was six. He'll graduate from there when he is seventeen and go to an institute which is what we would call a college.

At school he studies math, world history, geography, music, and painting. He also studies the Russian, Georgian, and English languages and literature. Misha could study German or Spanish but he chose English instead. Even though there are over one hundred languages spoken in the Soviet Union, every student must study Russian no matter which language is spoken at home.

Misha also attends a computer class. There are about forty students in this class and in most other classes as well. The room was filled with computers that were made in Japan.

In the gym I played basketball and soccer with Misha's friends. Soccer is very popular in Georgia. In Tbilisi there is a huge soccer stadium that seats eighty thousand people. Their home team is called Iveria and it has played teams all over the world.

Tennis and swimming are other popular sports in Georgia. There are many public tennis courts around the city. One day after school we played tennis at a public court. Misha won.

While visiting Misha's school I made lots of friends. At home it takes me a long time to make new friends. In Tbilisi, it took me only seconds.

We played freeze tag, hide and seek, and catch. One of the boys had a skateboard. We all took turns riding it and doing tricks. In Atlanta my friends and I also like to spend a lot of time skateboarding near school.

Another afternoon Shota invited me to go to the Chess House. The Chess House is a very large building where people come to practice and to play in tournaments. Chess is a very popular activity with children and adults. Shota told me that Georgian women are world chess champions.

While we were there I played a game of chess with Shota and I won!

On Thursday Buka surprised me by taking me to a video arcade after school. Before I left home all my friends wanted to know if I would find Nintendo games in the U.S.S.R. I didn't, but I had fun playing all the video games they did have.

In most of the homes I visited there were television sets. News was always on the stations but at certain hours I could watch cartoons. Even if I couldn't understand what the characters were saying, they still made me laugh because I could understand what they were doing.

One evening we went to a concert at the Children's Palace. I heard a men's chorus singing ancient Georgian folk songs in harmony. We also saw folk dancers depicting traditions of Georgian life. The dancing was very lively.

At the end of the week we were special guests at a Georgian feast. On the table were Georgian wine, *khachapuri* (flat bread with a cheese filling), *chakhokhbili* (chicken in sauce), *khinkali* (dumplings), beets, *chadi* (corn bread), and fruit.

Outside we could smell a bar-becue. Two men were grilling *mtsvadi* over a fire. Mtsvadi can be grilled lamb, pig, or young goat. That night it was lamb and it was delicious.

At every feast it is a Georgian custom to choose one man to be *tamada*. His job is to stand up and make toasts to the children, women, elders, and guests all during the meal. After each toast everyone says "Gaumarjos" which means cheers. By the time our feast was over our tamada had stood up over forty times. This made the feast very happy and very noisy.

After dinner some guests gathered around the piano and sang. Other guests danced. The Georgians love to sing and dance.

During the week Buka and I visited the spot where several Georgians were killed by Soviet troops on April 9, 1989. The Georgians were demonstrating for freedom and independence from the Soviet Union. Now people bring flowers and wreaths there every day. "Many republics are determined to have independence," Buka said.

The day before we left I told Buka about the seeds I had brought from Atlanta.

"I know the perfect place to plant them," Buka said. So he drove me to a hillside outside Tbilisi. On the hill there was a tree with many pieces of fabric tied to it. He called it a wishing tree and explained that each piece of cloth represented one wish. "Plant your seeds here and I am sure that they will grow. We will wish for friendship and understanding between our two countries." When we dug the dirt I noticed it was red just like the earth at home. Buka promised to check in a few weeks to see if the seeds had sprouted.

The day finally came for us to leave. I wore the Georgian outfit I had been given by Misha's family. Everyone thought I looked very Georgian.

I was very sad to say good-bye to all my new friends. They all promised to come visit us in Atlanta very soon.

Several months later Buka did come to stay in our home in Atlanta. The first thing he told me was that our seeds had grown.

Afterword

Joe Schulten's trip was the result of a simple idea that inspired his mother shortly after the Soviet-American summit talks failed in 1986. Leslie Schulten believed that the common citizen can make a difference, so she set about to get American and Soviet children to understand each other, even if their leaders couldn't. Naming her campaign Project Peace Tree, Leslie sought the cooperation of parents, teachers, principals, clergy, and businessmen from the Atlanta metropolitan area. Her goal was to accumulate thousands of friendship letters which were to be delivered to Soviet children as the first step toward an ongoing exchange.

As the campaign developed momentum, it gained the attention of Mayor Andrew Young of Atlanta, who proclaimed a Peace Tree Week and appointed Leslie as official delegate of the Atlanta-Tbilisi Sister City Committee. By the time Leslie delivered the first ten thousand letters to the Soviet Union, Project Peace Tree had put down strong roots in both Atlanta and Tbilisi. Since that simple beginning the Peace Tree Foundation has successfully completed the Face-to-Face life mask exchange, organized children's exchange visits between Atlanta and Tbilisi, and built a children's dental clinic in Tbilisi through the Georgian (U.S.S.R.) Children's Fund.

Guided by Leslie's dedication and spirit, the mission of the Peace Tree Foundation has evolved from making new friends to helping friends already made.